WINONA RYDER

A Real-Life Reader Biography

Valerie Menard

Mitchell Lane Publishers, Inc.
P.O. Box 619 • Bear, Delaware 19701

Mitchell Lane
PUBLISHERS

Copyright © 2001 by Mitchell Lane Publishers. All rights reserved. No part of this book may be reproduced without written permission from the publisher. Printed and bound in the United States of America.

First Printing

Real-Life Reader Biographies

Selena	Robert Rodriguez	Mariah Carey	Rafael Palmeiro
Tommy Nuñez	Trent Dimas	Cristina Saralegui	Andres Galarraga
Oscar De La Hoya	Gloria Estefan	Jimmy Smits	Mary Joe Fernandez
Cesar Chavez	Chuck Norris	Sinbad	Paula Abdul
Vanessa Williams	Celine Dion	Mia Hamm	Sammy Sosa
Brandy	Michelle Kwan	Rosie O'Donnell	Shania Twain
Garth Brooks	Jeff Gordon	Mark McGwire	Salma Hayek
Sheila E.	Hollywood Hogan	Ricky Martin	Britney Spears
Arnold Schwarzenegger	Jennifer Lopez	Kobe Bryant	Derek Jeter
Steve Jobs	Sandra Bullock	Julia Roberts	Robin Williams
Jennifer Love Hewitt	Keri Russell	Sarah Michelle Gellar	Liv Tyler
Melissa Joan Hart	Drew Barrymore	Alicia Silverstone	Katie Holmes
Winona Ryder	Alyssa Milano	Freddie Prinze, Jr.	Enrique Iglesias
Christina Aguilera			

Library of Congress Cataloging-in-Publication Data
Menard, Valerie.
    Winona Ryder/Valerie Menard.
        p. cm. — (A real-life reader biography)
    Filmography: p.
    Includes index.
    ISBN 1-58415-039-4
    1. Ryder, Winona, 1971- —Juvenile literature. 2. Motion picture actors and actresses—United States—Biography—Juvenile literature.[1. Ryder, Winona, 1971- 2. Actors and actresses. 3. Women—Biography.] I. Title. II. Series.
PN2287.R94 M46 2000
791.43'028'092—dc21
[B]
        00-034921

ABOUT THE AUTHOR: Valerie Menard has been an editor for *Hispanic* magazine since the magazine moved to Austin, Texas, in July 1994. Before joining the magazine, she was a managing editor of a bilingual weekly, *La Prensa*. Valerie writes from a Latino perspective and as an advocate for Latino causes. She is the author of several biographies for children including *Oscar De La Hoya*, *Cristina Saralegui*, and *Salma Hayek* (Mitchell Lane) and the author of the newly published *Latinos: Traditional Celebrations, Modern Realities* (Marlowe).

PHOTO CREDITS: cover: Archive Photos; p. 4 The Kobal Collection; p. 15 AP Photo; p. 17 The Kobal Collection; p. 19 Globe Photos; p. 21 The Kobal Collection; p. 22 Globe Photos; p. 27 AP Photo

ACKNOWLEDGMENTS: The following story has been thoroughly researched, and to the best of our knowledge, represents a true story. While every possible effort has been made to ensure accuracy, the publisher will not assume liability for damages caused by inaccuracies in the data, and makes no warranty on the accuracy of the information contained herein. This story is neither endorsed nor authorized by Winona Ryder.

Table of Contents

Chapter 1
An Eccentric Childhood

She's a member of a generation of children who were born in the seventies and who so confused their parents that adults called them Generation X. But that was unfair. Just because these children were confused, like most teenagers, and seemed a little more dark and moody than most kids, was no reason to put an "X" on a whole generation of kids, as if to pretend they didn't exist. Several tragic losses of young lives to violence, suicide, or drug abuse have marred this generation, but there's even more of which to be proud.

Winona is a member of Gener—ation X.

This is a generation of thinkers, children who have an adult view of the world. All they lack is the emotional maturity to understand it. They are also very creative and brave. Many young entertainers have emerged from this generation—one who captures its uniqueness more than most is Winona Ryder.

Born Winona Laura Horowitz on October 29, 1971, she was named after the Minnesota town, Winona, that was the place of her birth. Her parents later moved to northern California. Noni—her nickname—would consider Petaluma, California, her home town, but she would not be raised as a typical California girl.

She was born Winona Laura Horowitz on October 29, 1971.

In 1970, her parents, Cindy and Michael Horowitz, met and married in San Francisco, California. Cindy had been married before and had two children with her first husband: Winona's half-sister Sunyata, and half-brother, Jubal, both older than she. Winona also has a younger brother, Uri.

Her parents were free-thinking, intelligent individuals, who were open to new experiences. Cindy studied Buddhism and Michael collected and sold antique books. Because of this, Winona was encouraged early on to explore and most importantly, to ask questions.

Her parents also had a lifestyle that exposed them to many of the temptations facing young people today, including drugs. They were never drug addicts but they knew people who had experimented with them, including Timothy Leary, a professor who eventually gained fame in the sixties for his theory that recreational drug use was okay. Leary, who died in 1996, was Winona's godfather. With their background, her parents offered their children important information to keep them out of trouble. Winona told *Rolling Stone* magazine, "My parents know what it's like to, like, take a drug and go out in public and flip out. They always said, 'If you ever want to do anything,

Her parents were free-thinking individuals who were open to new experi— ences.

you just have to tell us about it, and you have to go through us.'" Winona feels it was this honesty from her parents that kept her from ever trying drugs, while many of her friends, unfortunately, did.

Her mother remembers that as a child, Winona showed an interest in learning and creativity. "She has a sense of identity that's pure and more self-confident than anyone else in the family, including her father and myself," she told a reporter for *Rolling Stone*. "I realized it when she was three or four. She went through materials so fast—drawing supplies, toys, books—you had to keep giving her stuff to keep her interested. She'd just consume them."

Surrounded by books, Winona was encouraged to read.

Surrounded by books, she was also encouraged to read. Books are a wonderful way for children to explore new places and to imagine new things. One of the first books that Winona read that influenced her was called *The Catcher in the Rye* (Bantam Books: New York, 1945) by J.D. Salinger. The book tells about the experiences of a teenage boy who is sent to boarding school. The main character, Holden Caulfield, fills the book with his views on people, politics, and life as a sixteen-year-old. Winona first read the book when she was only eight, but when she turned twelve, she read it again, and that's when the book's power hit her: "It became the Bible for me." Today, she owns a first-edition (one of the first copies published) of this book, among others.

Another reason that Winona learned to appreciate books was because when she was seven, her parents moved to what has been called a commune. In the sixties communes became very popular. In a commune, a group of people would live together, sometimes in separate houses, but usually on a ranch or a farm. They would form their own community and share chores to keep it going, like feeding the animals, cooking meals, or farming crops. In Winona's case, her parents moved to what she calls a suburb because it was

Her favorite book is *The Catcher in the Rye* by J. D. Salinger.

more like a neighborhood than a commune, although not a very fancy one. They didn't have electricity, so she didn't watch television. She and her friends would invent different games to play in order to have fun. "We'd have hammock contests, sit around and make up stories, make up weird games. I don't know—it was a weird, weird childhood. I mean it was great," she told *Rolling Stone*.

She may describe it as weird, but Winona also grew up with the same interests as many kids. Besides her love of books, she had a collection of Barbies, charm bracelets, and socks, and she even remembers her first crush. She was an avid Los Angeles Dodgers fan, and her favorite player was infielder Steve Sax. She even wrote "Winona Sax" on her notebook. She was crushed, however, when Sax left the Dodgers to join their rivals, the New York Yankees.

Acting was also something that Winona discovered she loved to do at an early age. When Winona was to enter junior high school, the family moved to Petaluma, California. Always an individual, she joined Amnesty International—an organization that works to free people who have been unfairly imprisoned for political reasons—she wore her hair short, and she dressed in baggy clothes. Moving from the commune to a small suburban town, Winona stuck out. Three days after she started school, several boys approached her at her locker. They thought she was a homosexual boy and beat her up. Too afraid to return to that school, Winona was allowed to stay home and her parents hired a tutor to teach her. For extracurricular activities, Winona's mother suggested she attend a theatrical school in San Francisco, the American Conservatory Theatre (ACT).

Life would improve quickly from then on. She enjoyed acting and by the time she finished the eighth grade, she had starred in her first movie and had gained a new name.

When she moved from the commune to a small suburban town, she was beat up at school.

Chapter 2
The First Hollywood Years

Winona had starred in six movies before she graduated from high school.

By the time Winona was ready to graduate from high school—with a 4.0 grade point average—she had already sold a movie script which she co-wrote, and starred in six movies. At seventeen, she would move out of her parent's house and into her own apartment in Los Angeles. She was already earning a good salary but hadn't reached the age where she could own a credit card. During one interview, she took a reporter along with her shopping and he watched as Winona pulled out one $100 bill after another to pay for her purchases.

Winona began the roller coaster ride of fame with her first film, *Lucas*.

While at the ACT, Winona was cast in several stage performances. One day, talent scout Deborah Lucchesi happened to catch one of these performances. She asked Winona to tape a screen test for the movie *Desert Bloom*, and when Lucchesi's bosses saw the tape, they signed Winona as a client. Although Winona was not cast in *Desert Bloom*, when director David Selzer saw Winona's tape, he immediately cast her in *Lucas*. Selzer explains his reaction to the tape in *Rolling Stone:* "There was Winona, this little frail bird. She had the kind of presence I had never seen—an inner life. Whatever message was being said by her mouth was being contradicted by her eyes."

Winona remembers the moment when she found out she got the part. She had just finished walking home from school—she enrolled in a different junior high school for a short time—and after getting home, somewhat

At the age of seventeen, Winona moved out on her own.

exhausted, her sister announced, "Oh, you got the part in that movie." Not only did she get the part, she also found a new name. When the film was about to be released, she was asked how she wanted her name to appear in the movie's credits. At that moment, she changed her name from Winona Horowitz to Winona Ryder. Although not exactly sure why she chose that name, she thinks it may have come from the name of one of her father's favorite singers, Mitch Ryder.

After *Lucas,* released in 1986, Winona starred in a second film that may be the only one of which she's not extremely proud, *Square Dance* (1987). But that was quickly followed up by her first real breakthrough movie, *Beetlejuice* (1988).

In this movie, she played a character that embodied the image of her generation—a girl obsessed with death and darkness, but more mature than the adults in her life. She co-starred in this movie with actors Michael

Keaton, Geena Davis, and Alec Baldwin.
Most importantly, she got the chance to
work with director Tim Burton, who
would go on to direct his biggest movies
so far, *Batman* and *Batman Returns*. She
would later make a second movie with

While Winona was filming Beetlejuice, she was tutored by studio teacher Linda Stone-Elster.

Burton, *Edward Scissorhands* (1990), where she would meet her first serious boyfriend, Johnny Depp.

She followed up *Beetlejuice* with a second breakthrough film, *Heathers* (1989). She co-starred with actor Christian Slater in this film which received a lot of attention because of its dark subject matter. In this film, Winona plays Veronica Sawyer, who happens to be a member of the popular set in high school, but because she has more integrity than her friends, she hates them for their shallowness. Her evil boyfriend, played by Slater, convinces her that her friends, who happen to all be named Heather, should die, and proceeds to kill them while making their deaths look like suicides. This role allowed Winona to expand from the wide-eyed innocent characters she had played to the darker, confused heroine who finds the strength to overcome her friends and most importantly, stop her boyfriend.

In 1990, she filmed *Edward Scissor-hands* where she met her first boyfriend, Johnny Depp.

More movies would follow: *Great Balls of Fire* (1989), *Welcome Home, Roxy Carmichael* (1990), *Mermaids* (1990), and *Night on Earth* (1991). Playing teenagers in a variety of roles made sense to Winona—after all, she was a teenager herself—but by the time she turned twenty, she was ready to become a woman, on screen and off.

Chapter 3
Playing a
Woman

Winona's first adult role was in _Age of Innocence._

As a nineteen-year-old, Winona Ryder had already accomplished so much. She had completed nine movies, begun her own production company, and had earned enough money to buy her first house—she had a whole room in the house set aside for her collection of J.D. Salinger first editions. Always ahead of her peers, Winona was ready for a change in focus. She had enjoyed a lot of success playing a teenager, but as she looked toward her twenties, she wanted to play a woman.

The first movie to give her this opportunity was called _Age of Innocence_

(1993). It co-starred Daniel Day-Lewis and Michelle Pfeiffer, and was directed by Martin Scorcese. In this movie, Winona played the young wife of Day-Lewis, but he falls in love with another woman. Critics were very impressed with her performance because it showed that she had the ability to express adult emotions and ideas through her character. She was rewarded with an Academy Award nomination and a Golden Globe award for Best Supporting Actress.

Winona (second from left) in Age of Innocence.

The next film would be a bit more dramatic: *Bram Stoker's Dracula* (1992) (*Age of Innocence* was released after *Dracula*, but filmed before it). The idea to do this film was hers, and she presented it to director Francis Ford Coppola at a meeting. She co-starred in this film with actors Gary Oldman and Keanu Reeves. This was Winona's first R-rated movie, more because of the violence than the sex—Winona refuses to do nude scenes in any film. *Dracula* would not be an easy project for her. In one instance, the director chose to verbally abuse her while she was completing a scene in order to get the right reaction from her. But the movie did establish her as a young woman who had moved on from teenager roles.

Winona quickly followed these projects with more movies, like *The House of the Spirits* (1994), a film version of the novel by Chilean novelist Isabel Allende, and *Reality Bites* (1994), which was produced by her production company. These pictures were followed by a film that had more personal significance to her, *Little Women* (1994).

In October 1993, a young girl, Polly Klaas, was kidnapped. Klaas happened to be from Winona's home town, so the case really struck home for Winona. While there was still hope that the girl was still alive, she felt that she had to do something to help find her. Once the news of the abduction broke, she got through to the Klaas family and offered her help, even posting a reward of $200,000. Sadly, Polly Klaas was murdered, but the family set up the Klaas Foundation to look for missing children. *Little Women*, written by Louisa May Alcott, was Polly's favorite book. Her parents gave Winona their daughter's copy of the book. Winona dedicated the movie to

Winona dedicated the movie Little Women *to Polly Klaas, a young girl who had been murdered in Winona's home town.*

Ethan Hawke, Winona Ryder, Janene Garofalo, and Steve Zahn starred in Reality Bites.

Polly. "To me, it really wasn't a cause," she explains to *Rolling Stone.* "It was like, 'This is an outrage and it's outrageous that more people aren't outraged.' When something happens to a child, the world should stand still."

Winona remains a girl of action, but more importantly, she maintains her principles and integrity despite the temptations she faces.

Chapter 4
Winona's Attitude

It's not surprising that Winona Ryder idolizes the character Holden Caulfield in the book *The Catcher in the Rye.* Like many young people, he was caught in a situation that was beyond his control—his parents sent him away to boarding school. But he manages to deal with the situation by using his intelligence, which helps him recognize the good and bad in everyone he meets. He has no patience for people who pretend to be something that they are not; he sees right through them. Winona is the same way. She looks for the truth in everything and everyone and that's

Winona's hero is Holden Caulfield from the book *The Catcher in the Rye.*

what has helped her to become such a talented actress.

When choosing which role to play, Winona is determined to find a part in which she believes. She's had good instincts so far, although there were times when the people around her thought she was making a huge mistake. When she chose to play Veronica in the movie *Heathers*, her agent at the time was so sure the film would hurt her career that she begged Winona not to do it. But Winona's instincts and conviction won out.

She considers herself an artist, and for that reason, she doesn't consider how much money a movie will make before she accepts a part. "To a true artist the career stuff shouldn't matter, but it matters to too many of those people who call themselves actors but are really just posers," she told *Rolling Stone.* "I'm thrilled if one of my movies is a hit. But you should do what hits you. If I'm in a movie and I'm not really into it, then I feel like I'm lying, and

When choosing which role to play, Winona is determined to find a part she believes in.

maybe other people will pick up on the fact that I'm lying."

Many times actors can get so caught up in their work and trying to live up to their fame, that they get cut off from the real world. Winona still ventures out in public as much as she can—one interview with a reporter took place at a flea market—and she still stays informed about important issues. She was once invited by another actor to go to a dinner party and meet President Bill Clinton. Although she declined, she does think it's important to get involved. "I think it's great for my generation to grow up politically active and do what they can for what they really believe in, but it has to be for something they know about, because so many times I hear actors talking about politics and I can tell that if someone asked them a question they probably wouldn't be able to answer it," she said in an article in *Esquire.*

Being famous carries a great responsibility and Winona accepts that,

She ventures out in public as much as she can, and she stays informed about important issues.

> **Winona is extremely sensitive. She can't stand to upset people or for people to think badly of her.**

although it makes her a little nervous. She knows that many young people look up to her, so she's careful not to make bad decisions. "Having people look up to me freaks me out. It's actually motivating because it makes me want to do a really good job." Besides the Klaas Foundation, she also joined the board of trustees for the American Indian College Fund, a nonprofit organization that raises funds to support the 30 tribal colleges in the U.S.

The life of an actor may seem to be ideal. Actors like Winona are very well paid. They can afford to buy a lot of fun things, eat at the best restaurants, and wear designer clothes. But Winona knows what it's like to be poor and she's very grateful for the success she's had. She's also critical of fellow actors who don't appreciate their good fortune. "For a long time, I was almost ashamed of being an actress," she told *Rolling Stone.* "I felt like it was a shallow occupation." When she sees other actors who choose to live as if they were poor, she gets mad. "It offends me, because I know what it's like to be in poverty, and it's not fun, and it's not romantic, and it's not cool."

Winona is also extremely sensitive. She says she's very insecure. She can't stand to upset people or for people to think badly of her. She also admits to working too hard, and early in her career she even suffered from insomnia. In 1993, her experiences after making one film combined with a personal crisis that forced her to ask for help.

In 1994, Winona won a Golden Globe Award for Best Supporting Actress in Age of Innocence.

Chapter 5
Girl Continues

In 1993, Winona's relationship with Johnny Depp fell apart.

Depression can be a serious illness. Help can come from doctors and medication, but like alcoholism, there is no cure, and fighting depression is a daily struggle.

Winona Ryder met her first love, Johnny Depp, at the young age of eighteen. The attraction was mutual—he was so crazy about her that he got a tattoo with the words "Winona Forever." Even though they got engaged, they never married. In 1993, her relationship to Depp fell apart, and at the same time, she was acting in one of her most difficult films, *The House of the Spirits.* Filmed in Portugal, the story deals with the downfall of a wealthy family who is caught in a political revolution. For that movie, Winona had to film a torture scene. By the time the filming was done, Winona was physically exhausted and emotionally depressed.

Her breakup with Depp and the work on *The House of the Spirits* had had a serious impact on Winona. At the time, she voluntarily checked into a psychiatric hospital for some rest. She only stayed five days, but she never forgot it. "I really got nothing from it. It didn't help me at all. But the thing that I did 'get' is that those places don't really help. You don't go to a place and get a pill that fixes you. They don't give you a sheet of secret answers. You can't pay enough money to have a place fix you," she told Bruce Kirkland of *The Toronto Sun.*

Years later, she happened to read a book about a young woman, Susanna Kaysen, who had a similar experience.

She filmed a very depressing movie, *The House of the Spirits.*

The book, *Girl, Interrupted*, is a true story about Kaysen's struggle with depression, which eventually landed her in a psychiatric hospital. Kaysen was seventeen at the time.

Kaysen's experience spoke to Winona. She felt it was an important film to make because it could help other teenagers who feel depressed. "Life is just weird. Life is a mess," she said. "I hope teenagers who feel alone out there will see this movie and say 'Thank God.' If I had seen this movie at nineteen, I would have taken a lot of comfort in it." The movie *Girl, Interrupted* was released in 1999.

In 2000, Winona released *Autumn in New York*, which co-starred Richard Gere. As for her personal life, she has met a new love, actor Matt Damon.

Winona Ryder has come a long way from the teen idol she used to be. She continues to grow as an actress and an artist, but most importantly, as a person.

In 2000, Winona starred with Richard Gere in *Autumn in New York*.

Filmography

Lucas (1986)
Square Dance (1987)
Beetlejuice (1988)
1969 (1988)
Heathers (1989)
Great Balls of Fire! (1989)
Welcome Home, Roxy Carmichael (1990)
Edward Scissorhands (1990)
Mermaids (1990)
Night on Earth (1991)
Bram Stoker's Dracula (1992)
Age of Innocence (1993)
Reality Bites (1994)
The House of the Spirits (1994)
Little Women (1994)
How to Make an American Quilt (1995)
Boys (1996)
Looking for Richard (1996)
The Crucible (1996)
Alien: Resurrection (1997)
Celebrity (1998)
Girl, Interrupted (1999)
Autumn in New York (2000)

Chronology

- 1971 Born October 29, in Winona, Minnesota
- 1983 re-reads *The Catcher in the Rye* by J.D. Salinger, which becomes her all-time favorite book
- 1985 is cast in her first film, *Lucas*
- 1988 makes the movie *Heathers* against the will of her advisers. The movie launches her career
- 1991 nominated for a Golden Globe award for Best Supporting Actress in *Mermaids*
- 1992 plays her first non-teenager in *Age of Innocence*
- 1992 breaks up with her first boyfriend and, suffering from exhaustion, checks into a psychiatric clinic
- 1993 wins a Golden Globe for Best Supporting Actress for *Age of Innocence*
- 1993 joins the search for kidnapped girl Polly Klaas
- 1994 *Reality Bites* becomes the first movie produced by her production company
- 1999 Releases *Girl, Interrupted*, which deals with mental illness
- 2000 Stars in *Autumn in New York* with Richard Gere

Index